# Breakthrough Thinking
# No Limits in God

PASTOR ANTHONY J. STEPHENSON

ISBN 978-1-68197-796-6 (Paperback)
ISBN 978-1-68197-797-3 (Digital)

Christian Faith Publishing, Inc.
296 Chestnut Street
Meadville, PA 16335
www.christianfaithpublishing.com

Printed in the United States of America

# ACKNOWLEDGMENT

I want to give special thanks to my wife Yolanda for all the love, support, and the work that she has provided me through all the different phases of ministry and even with the time she has put in with this book. Thank you also to my daughter and son-in-law Kanesha and Tony, and my two sons Anthony Jr. and An'tre. I am so proud of the love and support you all provide to me in the ministry and the vision as a whole. To the family of Life Changing International Church, I want to thank you for your faithfulness and your commitment to the ministry as the vision comes to pass.

And a special thanks to my mother Magdalene who is dear to my heart and without your prayers I wouldn't be where I am today, also to my late father, James Stephens, who taught me the importance of hard work and dedication, and to my spiritual father, Pastor Ronald Diggs. Of Word of Life Tabernacle, thank you for the wisdom that has contributed to this book.

# INTRODUCTION

In this book, you will see how people everywhere are experiencing different challenges in their lives, losing their jobs, not having enough finances, struggling families, having challenges in their marriage, rising divorce, the list goes on and on. Even though you live in this physical, natural world, which is governed and controlled by laws, there is another law that is not controlled by the laws of this land or the laws of this physical world called the law of thinking.

The law of thinking is a law that says what you constantly consistently think on will manifest in your life or will be your life (*see* Proverbs 23:7). Breakthrough thinking will come as a result of what you think on and how you process even that what you are going through. What is breakthrough? A breakthrough is an act or instance of breaking through an obstacle.

It was my lack of knowledge and understanding of spiritual laws that was the root to all I was encountering. God is no respecter of person. "Then Peter opened his mouth, and said, of a truth I perceive that God is no respecter of persons" (Acts 10:34).

It wasn't until I discovered this truth that if I wanted a breakthrough in my life, it must first start in my thinking as you read this prophetic book. "The eyes of your understanding being enlightened; that ye may know what is the hope of his calling, and what the riches of the glory of his inheritance in the saints" (Ephesians 1:18). I agree with you. From this day forward, you will no longer be in or brought into bondage in any way because of your breakthrough thinking!

# CHAPTER 1

# The Power of a Renewed Life

"Beloved, I wish above all things that thou mayest prosper and be in health, even as thy soul prospereth" (3 John 1:2).

Here is John an old man given wisdom that is the will of God, not much attention had been put to it. He said, "I wish, I pray, above all things." Wow, above all things, what does He wish that we have above all things, that we prosper and be in health even as the soul prospers.

Here is the key because we are talking about breakthrough thinking. He said, "Even as the soul, the mind, the will, the emotions, prosper." But there can't be no prosperity in the soul without the Word of God. Only the Word of God has the power to prosper you in your soul, body, spirit, health, finances, and all.

" So if you want to prosper Gods way, and breakout from the box this world has put us in (what we can or can't do), it's going to require a renewed mind. And the Word of God has all the tools to renew your mind. But the first thing you have to do is make a decision and be willing to stick with it. It's going to require a renewed way of thinking, concerning how you always done things. But the outcome of it will be unimaginable. Now let's look at what it means to be renewed. Renewed is to make new, or as if new again; restore: to start over again, to take up again; resume: renew (*see* 2 Corinthians 5:17).

Therefore, if any man in Christ He is a new creature altogether, all things have become new. This newness is not in the mind according to what you have already been taught by this world system. But this newness is in your spirit in your new life with God now; which is a whole new way of living that now exists.

But your natural mind has to be renewed from what you have already been taught and exposed to whether by some teaching, family environment, association, or just by your own perception how you may perceive something (*see* Mark 1:14–15).

Jesus's first message that He began to teach and preach in public was to repent for the kingdom heaven is at hand.

Repent, to think differently, have a change of mind, why? Because the kingdom that was once shut out to all is now being made available, but it's going to require a change in your thinking according to how you may have always done things (*see* Romans 12:1–3)

Paul is urging the Roman Church not to be conforming to this world but be transformed by the renewal of the mind; to be transformed is to have change in whatever is being transformed.

All transformation in any area of life will require change.

1. A mind-set is a fixed mental attitude or disposition that is responsible for our responses to the situations we face.
2. We are a product of what we think about most (Proverbs 23:7).
3. When we begin to have a kingdom mind-set, we begin to be conscious of the fact that God is our ruler, and He has a plan for us.
4. He wants to influence and impact our lives.
5. Everything derives from God. Therefore, we must know and understand His Word.
   (creflodollarministries.org)

There is power in a renewed mind. A person with a renewed mind can't be stopped by anything in this natural world. Breakthrough thinking is a way of thinking that causes an individual to break through any opposition that they face whether it's a job that has to be done in a short amount of time or something such as persecution, financial strain, and health issues. When you have a breakthrough thinking that person will be difficult to break under any pressure. Breakthrough thinking is the mindset you must have in this twenty-first century, especially all that is constantly been thrown at you every day all day through the Internet, television, radio, billboards, and economy plus so many other things that there is not enough time to mention. But when you renew your mind with the Word of God, you now have the mind of Christ, which is already an overcoming mindset.

A renewed mind is one of the most powerful possessions you can have in this Earth. I personally did not realize how my thinking and speech were so limited because I was just doing what society trained me to do. Now my mother and grandmother, they were at that time the only people whom I had seen with my own eyes walk in and give an unconditional love to everyone they came into contact with. My mind-set was I couldn't see my self-doing that because my thinking was no one was going to get over on me, or use me, or if anything, I was going to get them before they got me.

That's why Paul is urging us in Romans 12:2, "Be not conformed to this world" because the truth is this world system is a system that is already set up. Look around you, you can go and get yourself a four-year degree and really work hard to get it but then come out and can't find a job. You think of the veterans who served in wars and risked their lives every day for our country only to come back home having to struggle just to get needs met or sadly end up homeless. I am in no way blaming the economy or anyone in any kind of office regarding the condition of the land. What my focus is on is it doesn't matter who you are, where you come from, and what life you once lived, if you learn the power of a renewed mind, that alone can put you in places that you never thought you could reach and bring people into your life that you thought you would never meet. "For as he thinketh in his heart, so is he: Eat and drink, saith he to thee; but his heart is not with thee" (Proverbs 23:7).

What you continually give your thoughts to you will become, whether its good, bad, positive, negative, rich, or poor. These are laws that have already been established since the foundation of the world. The mind is very powerful; your mind will allow you to set, to embrace prosperity in your spirit, soul, and body. "Beloved, I wish above all things that thou mayest prosper and be in health, even as thy soul prospereth" (3 John 1:2).

Or your mind will reject it. That is all based upon what information you feed it first or come into the knowledge of something different than what you were exposed to. A process of thinking that keep you in bondage to so many things because you feel like you had to deal with it until you found another source of information, which is called the Word of God that removes the limitation and put you into a whole new level of thinking and living. – That's Breakthrough Thinking

> IF THEN you have been raised with Christ [to a new life, thus sharing His resurrection from the dead], aim at and seek the [rich, eternal treasures] that are above, where Christ is, seated at the right hand of God. [Ps. 110:1.] And set your minds and keep them set on what is above (the higher things), not on the things that are on the earth. For as far as this world is concerned you have died, and your new, life is hidden with Christ in God. When Christ, who is our life, appears, then you also will appear with Him in [the splendor of His] glory. So kill (deaden, deprive of power) the evil desire lurking in your members [those animal impulses and all that is earthly in you that is employed in sin]: sexual vice, impurity, sensual appetites, unholy desires, and all greed and covetousness, for that is idolatry (the deifying of self and other created things instead of God). (Colossians 3:1–5 AMP)

"There is a 'rest' that God has made available for believers today, but this rest is not referring to physical rest but an inward attitude—a complete trust in God. We rest in Him by trusting in everything He has accomplished for us through Jesus." (Quoted byPastor Creflo Dollar). When you renew your mind to the Word of God, there is a rest and peace that this world can't give it and this world can't take it away.

Peace is something that passes all understanding that shall keep your mind and heart through Christ Jesus. To have a renewed mind, it's going to require a lot of work, such as looking at things that expands your thinking. Talking and spending time with people to challenge you to come out of your comfort zones, now that will be the challenging part to some people because it's easier and more comfortable to be around people that let you remain the same and don't challenge you to change. But you have to ask yourself how much do you really want change in your life because if you don't have any motivation you will not stick with your initial plan. You will be surprised by things that you will start enjoying, comparing them to how you originally thought about it after you renew your mind. Renewing the mind is a powerful thing; there can be no change on the outside until there is a change on the inside, and that's what makes it so powerful because you are not subject to the things that goes on around you. When your thinking is different, your life will be different as well.

# CHAPTER 2

# Winning in Life

Winning is to be successful or victorious in (a contest or conflict, to win in an endeavor, to accomplish). When every boy or girl is born into this world, the hands they first come into contact with are not only their parent's hands, but the parents mind set as well. So no one comes into this Earth with the control of their future. The only thing they have is whom they go home with from the hospital. And now their future will begin, and there are three forces in the Earth that is trying to frame their world.

1. Parents, loved ones, and those who they are around everyday
2. Environments: neighborhoods, childhood friends, TV, music, etc.
3. School System: the school system is a combination of number one and two and even if they are trying to teach children how to live in society, there are still differences between the individual's home life and the environments they are exposed to.

The purpose of this book is to reach people on different levels of life regardless of what environment they come from. There is a victorious spirit in every one of us. Some may have already been taught it and understand it, and then there are others who have no idea or was never told that a winner is inside them.

No one started out in life with losing in mind. Even as children when playing a sport, they play that sport with winning in mind. But as you grow in life, things begin to happen that causes them to start to experience disappointments and letdowns and things not turning out like you thought they should, and slowly but surely, Satan is stealing confidence little by little - that winning (refusal to quit) attitude that you once use to protect.

St. John 10:10 AMP states, "The thief comes only in order to steal and kill and destroy. I came that they may have and enjoy life, and have it in abundance (to the full, till it overflows)." This was one of the assignments that Jesus came to fulfill and carry out. But it is also the assignment that Satan still has. Knowing and understanding what Jesus did is still more powerful and real than what Satan still tries to do. Winning in life has to become a mindset and the final authority. In other words, make a decision that nothing is bigger, stronger, and more real to you than the Word of God. But in order to get to that point, the Word of God will have to become a necessity, not an option.

> Now it came to pass, as they went, that he entered into a certain village: and a certain woman named Martha received him into her house. And she had a sister called Mary, which also sat at Jesus' feet, and heard his word. But Martha was cumbered about much serving, and came to him, and said, Lord, dost thou not care that my sister hath left me to serve alone? Bid her therefore that she helps me. And Jesus answered and said unto her, Martha, Martha, thou art careful and troubled about many things: But one thing is needful: and Mary hath chosen that good part, which shall not be taken away from her. (St Luke 10:38–42).

The key to that story is Jesus made it known how serving was good and wanting to feed them was great, but there is one thing that is needful, and he wasn't going to allow her, which was doing the needful thing which was sitting at His feet to go and do something that can wait. It makes this story so vital and important because as people, there is a tendency to put other things that we call important in front of what Jesus said was the needful thing. "He replied, it has been written, Man shall not live and be upheld and sustained by bread alone, but by every word that comes forth from the mouth of God [Deuteronomy 8:3.]" (Matthew 4:4 AMP).

It has been proven over and over again by men and women. The Word of God makes a difference in your attitude when you have or have not spent time with it. In your way of thinking concerning victory or defeat in your daily activities concerning energy and loss of energy, joy or no joy, peace or no peace, and happiness or no happiness, it has been proven that what Jesus told Martha still applies today.

To win in life is not only to have a mind that is set on winning, but winning must be in your mouth, "A man's belly shall be satisfied with the fruit of his mouth; and with the increase of his lips shall he be filled. Death and life are in the power of the tongue: and they that love it shall eat the fruit thereof" (Proverbs 18:20–21).

"For he that will love life, and see good days, let him refrain his tongue from evil, and his lips that they speak no guile" (1 Peter 3:10).

Since I understand that death and life are both in the power of my tongue, I will also eat the fruit of what's coming out of my mouth. I have to be very mindful of the life I desire, and the days I desire to see, what's coming out of my mouth will play the ultimate role of the experiences of my life concerning winning or living a life of defeat.

Challenges come to every individual on this Earth, but when you have a winning attitude; it causes that which seems to be so big to become so small. That's why this mentality has been hidden because when your eyes have become open to the fact, it doesn't matter what life you once lived or what wrong decisions you made in the past. But once you come to the knowledge and make a quality decision that you are a winner and not a loser even though some things may have failed in your life, you are not a failure but a winner. So every day, you must make a daily confession that this day you win over every situation and circumstances you face today. And you will enjoy this day that you already have victory over.

> But thanks be to God, Who gives us the victory [making us conquerors] through our Lord Jesus Christ. Therefore, my beloved brethren, be firm (steadfast), immovable, always abounding in the work of the Lord [always being superior, excelling, doing more than enough in the service of the Lord], knowing and being continually aware that your labor in the Lord is not futile [it is never wasted or to no purpose]. (1 Corinthians 15:57–58 AMP)

"Now thanks be unto God, which always causeth us to triumph in Christ, and maketh manifest the Saviour of his knowledge by us in every place" (2 Corinthians 2:14).

As you can see through the scriptures, God has already obligated and committed Himself to our success in life. That's why He encourages us in 1 Corinthians 15:58 to always do our best and do it with excellence. He also said do more than enough in your service, but that's where the trouble can come in at times because in this world, the world says, "I'm only doing just enough according to what I'm being paid and no more," or "I'm not going to be doing all that and not get no recognition for it." So there are many reasons why people don't do more than enough, not realizing or understanding that God's way is perfect, faultless proof that can't fail.

"As for God, his way is perfect: the word of the Lord is tried: he is a buckler to all those that trust in him" (Psalms 18:30).

So if you get this in your heart and your mind and make a decision that you can win in every situation you're up against, knowing the promises of God, the key is your faith, your belief, and confidence, which are not based upon your ability. It's based upon the promises of God. In order to have a breakthrough in your thinking, you must understand winning in life is not impossible actually it is the will of God.

You have been authorized by God to win; the devil is already defeated and has already been put under your feet. "Behold, I give unto you power to tread on serpents and scorpions, and over all the power of the enemy: and nothing shall by any means hurt you" (Luke 10:19).

So every day, make a daily confession that this day you are walking and living in the victorious power of God. You are winning in every area of your life. You have victory today over any adversity and walk in total victory in Jesus's name.

Winning in life will first start with an attitude that you win not from a bragging or thinking more of yourself but from the standpoint you are now in Christ and old things have passed away. One of the greatest hindrances for all of us are focusing on the past or letting our past mistakes and failures cause a fear to come in and stop us from pursuing the dream in our heart. But when we develop a winning attitude, one door can close, but we know another one will open. A winning attitude produces a confidence in us that all things are possible and it gets rid of the mindset or attitude of failure. And The truth is we don't have to win at everything to have a winning attitude, what a winning attitude does is give us a sense of accomplishment that if we don't win this one, we will win the next one. It causes a consistency to be in us not to quit.

Not everyone accepts the idea of a person that has a winning attitude is because society has instilled in people you can't win every time. Even a boxer can fall; the greatest football or basketball player can lose his game. That's not what I am talking about. I am talking about an attitude, a mindset that you can lose every time, but you never give up. Every successful man you talked to in life will tell you they had many failures before they found their click. I call it a click because when something clicks, something happen. But through it all, they never gave up. Even after being turned down, they didn't quit. We live in times now where we don't see much success as the men of old. There are many names I can call whose books are still very inspiring, but the difference is that they learned laws and stuck with them until they manifested. Today's society is learning the same laws but not willing to stick with the process until it shows up. That's what you call patience. A word many don't like to hear. But to a have a winning attitude, it requires patience, not arrogance but patience. Winning in life is also contagious. You will find when people come around you, your environment will be so full of life; joy can't help but to be there. This winning in life will give you a whole new perspective in life. The things that used to bother you, you will find that it was a waste of time because you have winning on your mind, winning in your marriage, winning in your family's life, winning in your business, and winning in your finances. Make a decision every day that this day is a winning day in every area of your life. Start your day with a confession, "This is the day which the Lord hath made; we will rejoice and be glad in it. Save now, I beseech thee, O Lord: O Lord, I beseech thee, send now prosperity" (Psalms 118:24–25).

And I know you are probably saying, "I don't know if I can do that, or "That seems like a lot to do." But you will be surprised when you expose your mind and body to something different, how they respond to it and eventually will start letting you know when you haven't done it.

Remember breakthrough thinking has no limits, so set your mind on that and keep it set.

# CHAPTER 3

# Living the Victorious Life, Overcoming the Spirit of Contentment

When it comes to living a victorious life, I am not talking about big homes, cars, big bank accounts, and a life full of stuff because having a lot of things will not bring you true success and true happiness. This victorious life that I am speaking of is a life of victory, not letting what you don't have get the best of you and cause you to act and do things that can cost you your life or someone else's or just no peace, all because you are trying to obtain something that you don't have.

And when it comes to contentment, some people settle in life far below their potential to do better or become greater at what they do. But the spirit of contentment will cause you not to push forward and go after what you really desire. To be successful or have success in anything whether it's a marriage, family, business, home, etc., it takes work, determination, and commitment to see it through, through the good times, challenging times, and discouraging times. When you look at people who may have a successful ministry, business, etc., they all will tell you the same thing that they had to pay a price to be where they are.

Contentment is to be content, is to be satisfied where you are at and what you have and desiring no more than what one has to be satisfied. And the danger to this contentment is you could have much more to give and to offer. I have discovered that most people live life by their environment, family traits, what others may say about them, or an inspiration that can come from someone else. And They never really discover the greatness within. This book is all about inspiring someone to live, live the life you desire to live instead of living the life society said you should live or how you can live.

With that attitude or mindset, you will not think it's necessary to change or make changes because to you, you are all right, knowing within yourself there's so much more you want to experience and have in your life. That comes from the fear of losing the people around you whom you have grown to love because if their attitude is one way, and you in the past has been that way yourself. But then you come to a place in life where you want more out of your life than what you have been doing. That means it's going to require breakthrough thinking.

This contentment isn't exactly the kind of happiness that someone has where you have a need for nothing; it's more like a peaceful ease of mind. It's being satisfied with what you have, whatever that is in spite of the despair that you are experiencing with it, refusing to change, in other words willing to suffer where you are instead of the pain of progress (*see* Jeremiah 29:11)

God says he has a plan for you, thoughts of peace and not of evil to give you an expected end. And you know if God has a plan for you, it has to be a great plan, a plan that not only will bring joy to you but also joy, peace, and happiness to others. That's always the plan of God.

"The thief comes only in order to steal and kill and destroy. I came that they may have and enjoy life, and have it in abundance (to the full, till it overflows)" (St. John 10:10 AMP).

God makes it plain the life He desires for us to live to the point that He sent Jesus to give His life in order that we may have and enjoy life. That alone lets you see it is important to God how you live, but God is no respecter of persons. One thing God will not do is override your will. So He has made everything available for you to live a good life, but it's going to first start with how you think. Your way of thinking is the beginning of something great or the ending of something that could have been great. It all starts with your thinking. In 2 Corinthians 8:9 AMP, He gave up what he had so that you might come up where he is.

"For you are becoming progressively acquainted with and recognizing more strongly and clearly the grace of our Lord Jesus Christ (His kindness, His gracious generosity, His undeserved favor and spiritual blessing), [in] that though He was [so very] rich, yet for your sakes He became [so very] poor, in order that by His poverty you might become enriched (abundantly supplied)" (2 Corinthians 8:9 AMP).

This is the love that our Heavenly Father has for us. You are experiencing hurt, pain, and disappointments; those are not His will for you (*see* Matthew 6:31–33 AMP). Seek at, aim, and strive after first of His entire kingdom, His way of doing and being right. It is the will of God that you seek and strive for the better He has for you.

All He wants all of us to do is get Him involved in our life, and you do that through reading, meditating, praying, and attending a place of worship where you can get taught how to walk with Him or how to live out the promises He has made available to you. God has already promised us that He will take care of us.

Paul is letting us know he learned to be content in whatever state that he is in. For the sake of the assignment, he learned many things will come, but it's not going to stop him. That has to become your attitude as many things come in life. But just because something comes that doesn't give it the right to stop or hinder where you are headed. How you view your challenges will automatically give you victory over them, or it gives them victory over you. In Philippians 4:9–13, He is not telling you to be content in your state but understand it's only a temporary situation that's got to change.

Timothy is urging the people that those teachers that was teaching about gain is proof of godliness, but they are teaching it for their own benefit then he said stay away from them. Why? Godliness with contentment is great gain. You know how you are living, and you trust God and you don't have to run after things you run after God. When going after God, He will make sure every need will be met, every desire fulfilled, and your days will be like heaven on earth (see 1 Timothy 6:3–10).

"That your days may be multiplied, and the days of your children, in the land which the Lord swore unto your fathers to give them, as the days of heaven upon the earth" (Deuteronomy 11:21).

"For the Lord God is a sun and shield: the Lord will give grace and glory: no good thing will he withhold from them that walk uprightly" (Psalms 84:11).

God made us a promise that no good thing will he withhold from those who walk up right. That's why he is urging his people to change their thinking and not to be like Israel. Israel was in Egypt for so long. They had an Egyptian mentality and didn't know how to be free. They were free people, but they were not free in their minds. Many people today are busy in life going to work, and coming home to their families, going to church with smiles on their faces, and saying they are blessed and highly favored, but there is a World War II going on in their heads. That means they need a breakthrough in their thinking.

You are the prophet of your life, the life you desire. Get the Word of God on it, and since His Word will not return to him, it shall accomplish that what He please and prosper in the place He sent it (see Isaiah 55:11). Find yourself a scripture; many of them have already been given to you. Take those scriptures and put them in your mouth and on your mind day and night like God told Joshua, and build an image of that Word in your heart and let God bring that Word into manifestation like he did with Jesus and Mary.

The spirit of contentment can also come through the mouths of other people, and the truth is that is Satan number one avenue he uses first, especially if it is someone you love and trust, and because you trust them and trust what they say. But the thing about it is how do you know that they have settled in life and not trying to move forward? You can know because that's all you continually hear them talk about, it's always a negative statement or comment when you or someone else talks about doing something new or moving forward in something or for instance you're thinking about moving into another house.

The spirit of contentment always makes you think, "This is as far as I need to go." So whenever you hear those voices, you don't have to compete with it or argue about it or anything, just know some things you just got to learn, who you can share things with, and who you can't. Nothing should be against the individual because every person has that right to determine how far he or she wants to go in life. All I'm suggesting is not to let someone else's limitation become yours or don't let someone else contentment become yours. But you set your goals, and you continue to trust God for what you desire in your life.

The spirit of contentment also wants you to settle right where you are at, nothing more or nothing less. Think about it for a minute as life goes on, and different needs come and that's just a part of life. And that's why God has given us His Word, His promise, His Holy Spirit, that no matter what comes in life, you as his child will always be taken care of. In the eyesight of God, he never wants to see you or I live like the world because the world doesn't represent Him and what he stands for. So it's really like a slap in his and Jesus's face for them to go through all they went through so you can forever be taken care of, and you say by the spirit of contentment, "I'm fine I don't want nothing else." And even if you don't want anything else, it is also fine because that's your right. So believe for more than enough so you can be a blessing to other people. Don't let the spirit of contentment rob you of the abundant life God has already prepared for you, and don't let it rob you from being a blessing to other people.

## CHAPTER 4

# The Power of Words

When it comes to breakthrough thinking, one of the most powerful tools to use concerning any breakthrough in your life is having the understanding of the power of words. Words are powerful forces that changes and rearranges things. From the very beginning of time, it was what God spoke that causes creation to come into being.

> Either make the tree good, and his fruit good; or else make the tree corrupt, and his fruit corrupt: for the tree is known by his fruit. O generation of vipers, how can ye, being evil, speak good things? For out of the abundance of the heart the mouth speaketh. A good man out of the good treasure of the heart bringeth forth-good things: and an evil man out of the evil treasure bringeth forth-evil things. But I say unto you, that every idle word that men shall speak, they shall give account thereof in the Day of Judgment. For by thy words thou shalt be justified, and by thy words thou shalt be condemned. (Matthew 12:33–37)

Jesus is letting it be known that by your words, you will be justified, acquitted, and brought into right standing with God, or by your words, you will be condemned or sentenced to death. Wow, look at that. How powerful words are. And we have been trained to say anything and talk anyway we want to, not realizing all those words are either creating something, making something better, or destroying something.

"Thou art snared with the words of thy mouth, thou art taken with the words of thy mouth" (Proverbs 6:2),

The wrong words coming out of your mouth will cause bondage to be in your life. So if you feel like you are in bondage in anyway—relationship wise, church wise, or family environment, back track and see what's been coming out of your mouth concerning that situation.

"And, behold, a woman, which was diseased with an issue of blood twelve years, came behind him, and touched the hem of his garment: For she said within herself, If I may but touch his garment, I shall be whole. But Jesus turned him about, and when he saw her, he said, Daughter, be of good comfort; thy faith hath made thee whole. And the woman was made whole from that hour" (Matthew 9:20–22)

She kept saying to herself if she can only touch the hem of his garment, she knows she will be healed. She kept saying even in the midst of the crowd, she kept saying. The outcome, she got is what she kept saying.

From the very beginning of time since creation took place, God spoke, and God said and God said and God saw what He said.

What I discovered is when a person is struggling with something or even with someone and there seems like an unending battle going on in the mind, the hardest thing to do is to speak the Word of God. But the question is why is that? It is because Satan knows when that word leave your mouth in faith, it's over, so his tactic is to overwhelm you with so much you don't have a desire to read the Bible, speak the Word, or even pray. That's why you have to make a decision. What if you can't get to the pastor or a brother or a sister in Christ, and you are all alone and the pressure is coming at you so fast, you don't have time to think, and you feel your body getting weaker and weaker like you have nothing else inside you to fight. That is when the revelation of breakthrough thinking has to come into play and remember the power of your words.

> Words are not just for the purpose of communicating with others although they do serve as a means of communication between people. The primary purpose for words is to create things. God is the originator of all creation, and the Word of God says that this world was created through His Word (Hebrews 11:3). As offspring of God, created in His image and likeness, we are supposed to be using our words to call those things that be not as though they were and pull unseen things out of the spiritual realm into the natural realm. However, we must grab hold of the fact that words are spiritual containers that carry faith or fear. When you speak the Word of God, you release the faith and power of God into the atmosphere of this earth and create an avenue through which the grace of God can flow into circumstances and situations.(Quoted by Pastor Creflo Dollar)

Words good or bad when spoken, that's what a lot of people have not been aware of, positive or negative, they will turn on the law of life or the laws of death. Watching what you say is not about being spiritual from the negative. It's about you having an understanding of the power of your words and the effect those words will have on your life.

"For verily I say unto you, That whosoever shall say unto this mountain, Be thou removed, and be thou cast into the sea; and shall not doubt in his heart, but shall believe that those things which he saith shall come to pass; he shall have whatsoever he saith" (Mark 11:23).

Jesus makes a promise that whatever you speak, don't doubt in your heart but believe that those things you say shall come to pass.

You shall have whatever you say. What a powerful promise. Now here is where your confidence comes to play, you already have a promise from God, He already told me you have nothing to fear.

He has me, and he will keep me from every hurt, harm, or danger. But one thing we must do like God said in Joshua 1:8, "This book of the law shall not depart out of thy mouth; but thou shalt meditate therein day and night, that thou mayest observe to do according to all that is written therein: for then thou shalt make thy way prosperous, and then thou shalt have good success."

We must keep the Word in our mouth day and night. Don't just start speaking the Word of God when faced with a challenge or when something arises that we need immediate help in. We must make the power of Words a part of our daily lives, so we can live a victorious life.

Words are more powerful than the thoughts we give to it. Words carry life or death. We have been trained to say just anything we want to say, not realizing that's been the greatest hindrance in all our lives. I remember when I first got born again, I was on fire for the Lord. In the word, all the time I couldn't get enough of the word. But for some reason, it's seems as if things were getting worse before they were getting better, and I cried out to God because I knew it wasn't supposed to be this way, and he revealed two things to me that forever changed my life.

1. That all the church services I was attending, and all the praying I was doing, and all the reading I was doing, and constantly reading all the time, but there was one thing I wasn't doing which was releasing my faith. Speaking it out of my mouth, I was filling my heart with it. But I was talking like everybody I was around because I didn't want anyone to say, "I've changed and now I'm spiritual," so instead of speaking what was in me, I was speaking like those around me.

2. "For the law of the Spirit of life in Christ Jesus hath made me free from the law of sin and death" (Romans 8:2).

I was not aware that there are laws that governed this Earth, and laws are activated by words. So every time I said I didn't have enough, it was never enough. Every time I cough and said, "I must be catching the flu," the law of sin and death are at work. But when I learned I owe no man but to love him, I'm already healed, and I'm already blessed, the spirit of life in Christ went to work. Both of those laws work day and night, fulfilling what's coming out of your mouth. Praise God we already have victory, and Satan has already been defeated. This is why we have to have a breakthrough in our thinking of lack, failure, sickness, and disease. We are already blessed, and it cannot be reversed.

# CHAPTER 5

# Overcoming the Spirit of Fear

"For God hath not given us the spirit of fear; but of power, and of love, and of a sound mind" (2 Timothy 1:7). The apostle Paul, being young Timothy's mentor and spiritual father, has given him some vital, critical words of wisdom. As the apostle Paul has aged and has experienced much opposition, he is letting young Timothy know in advance on the road that he is on that there will be times where that spirit of fear will approach him, and he is questioned whether or not he will be able to carry out the will of God or not. That attack starts in the mind because if he (Satan) can get you to think of defeat, you will already be defeated. If he can get you to think of failure, you've already failed. If he can get you to think whatever you are trying to accomplish is not going to work, you will never put forth action to see if it will work or not. But Paul admonished Timothy, "God has not given you the spirit of fear, but of power and of love and of a sound mind."

According to Genesis 1:26, God created man in his image and in his likeness, so in mankind is a built-in creator. In other words, inside man is the ability and capability to accomplish anything he sets his mind to do. But here is the danger of fear. Fear shuts down that creation side of you by making you think you can't do what appears to be beyond your comprehension. Fear will never allow you to step out and up to the fullness of your potential. The question is where did fear come from and how does it show up in an individual life?

1. Fear's origin is from Satan himself, to cause you to feel less than or afraid of your ability that you are not good enough.
2. Somewhere in your life, someone sowed a seed of fear in you. It could be fearful of giving because you don't know if you will have enough for you to meet your needs. Being fearful is not to trust someone because everybody is out to get you somehow. You are fearful of the dark because of horror stories you have been told or have even watched on television. Fear has constantly been pumped in our society every day everywhere.

Fear is a spirit that traps you in a place that will not allow you to move forward in life. It could be fear of stepping out in a business or fear of not knowing how the bills will get paid. Some are fearful of trusting someone because of what someone else has done. Fear will cause you to shut down the creative power that God has put in you. Fear is a grip that Satan uses to stop your faith from working.

But the scripture says God did not give us that spirit, but God has given us power, love, and a sound mind. So today, declare that you are free from the spirit of fear, and you have power, love, and a sound mind concerning every area of your life.

"Yea, though I walk through the valley of the shadow of death, I will fear no evil: for thou art with me; thy rod and thy staff they comfort me" (Psalms 23:4).

This is the master key that give you the advantage over this world where you don't have to fear because God is with you. Knowing that alone causes a breakthrough in your thinking where you no longer have to be fearful or afraid of anything or even anybody.

Psalms 27:1 says, "The LORD is my light and my salvation—whom shall I fear? The LORD is the stronghold of my life—of whom shall I be afraid?"

Psalm 118:6 says, "The LORD is with me; I will not be afraid. What can man do to me?" So when fear tries to step in and causes you to be fearful, you open your mouth and shout and declare, "No fear here." You are bold as a lion (*see* Proverbs 28:1). And walk in your freedom that Christ purchased for you on Calvary. We always win.

"There is no fear in love. But perfect love drives out fear, because fear has to do with punishment. The one who fears is not made perfect in love" (1 John 4:18).

Fear has torment that comes with it, and by that alone, our Father God does not want that spirit anywhere around us for one. St. John 10:10 says, "The thief cometh not, but for to steal, and to kill, and to destroy: I am come that they might have life, and that they might have it more abundantly."

It is the will of God that we not only have life but enjoy our life. "The thief comes only in order to steal and kill and destroy. I came that they may have and enjoy life, and have it in abundance (to the full, till it overflows)" (John 10:10 AMP).

And Being tormented by fear in anyway robs you of the abundant life that he wants us to have. Today, I am standing with you that fear will not rob you of the abundant life. I agree with you this day that you have already been delivered from past hurtful relationships, past failures, past mistakes, and wrong decisions and choices you may have made in the past that tried to keep you in bondage. You are free right now because the blood of Jesus has already made you free. The next step is no condemnation and say, "I will not walk around with condemnation and will not let people condemn me. I just got to know I'm free from the past, free from fear, free from failure, and free from people."

"Be strong and courageous. Do not be afraid or terrified because of them, for the LORD your God goes with you; he will never leave you nor forsake you" (Deuteronomy 31:6).

"Yea, though I walk through the valley of the shadow of death, I will fear no evil: for thou art with me; thy rod and thy staff they comfort me" (Psalms 23:4).

"For, you did not receive a spirit that makes you a slave again to fear, but you received the Spirit of son-ship. And by him we cry, 'Abba,' Father" (Romans 8:15).

"Now unto him that is able to do exceeding abundantly above all that we ask or think, according to the power that worketh in us" (Ephesians 3:20).

Here, God is letting us know that he is able to do exceedingly and abundantly above all that we ask or even think. In other words, you can't think high enough for God. But here is the key according to the power at work in you. So what is at work in you, how far can you see, and how high can you think? It's important to you that God wants to give you the life you can only dream about. But the spirit of contentment will always talk you into settling far less than what our Father God has already prepared for you. And because he is subtle and clever, he will make it seem like what you are doing is the will of God. For example, you got that one car that gets you to and fro where you need to be. You really don't need to believe God for another one because that one is getting the job done. But what about if they just called you from school concerning your child, and you go in a hurry to get there but come to find out the battery is dead and no one is home or around to help you, what are you going to do then? And that's what the spirit of contentment do, it over exaggerates anything of excess that you have to try to make you feel materialistic, and the whole while, he is working on a plan to cause depression, oppression, frustration, and it all comes from not having enough of anything at the time you need it most. Jesus Christ came and died to give us the life the father desires for us to have. But that spirit of religion and tradition has robbed many of God's people of this victorious life that has already been made and available for us. The purpose of this book is to bring people out of bondage and an Egypt mentally even though you may not be where you want to be, but you are not where you used to be. So I am challenging every born-again believer to remove all limitations and trust the God of Abraham, Isaac, and Jacob. His Word still has miracle- working power in it. His Word is still healing; His Word is still delivering people. There is no reason any of us should be content about anything. We have a Father that knows how to take care of His children. We are so blessed as a people as a nation. The victorious life is yours now, not tomorrow, or when you think you got it all together. It's yours now. Walk in your victory, speak in victory, and let Jesus be magnified in your life.

# CHAPTER 6

# No Limits

A limit is a point beyond which is not possible to go, a point beyond which someone is not allowed to go, something that bounds, restrains or confined, stop or prevent the increase in something or someone. –Dictionary.com

A limit is a boundary that is already set that says you can't go any further. That's why the spirit of God gave this book to me, to break that boundary and mindset that hinder God from fulfilling all He desires to do in your life. But because God will never override your will, He has given you promises to live by, that will move you from that land of limitations, but it first starts with your thinking.

> And they returned from searching of the land after forty days. And they went and came to Moses, and to Aaron, and to all the congregation of the children of Israel, unto the wilderness of Paran, to Kadesh; and brought back word unto them, and unto the entire congregation, and showed them the fruit of the land. And they told him, and said, we came unto the land whither thou sentest us, and surely it floweth with milk and honey; and this is the fruit of it. Nevertheless the people be strong that dwell in the land, and the cities are walled, and very great: and moreover we

saw the children of Anak there. The Amalekites dwell in the land of the south: and the Hittites, and the Jebusites, and the Amorites, dwell in the mountains: and the Canaanites dwell by the sea, and by the coast of Jordan. And Caleb stilled the people before Moses, and said, Let us go up at once, and possess it; for we are well able to overcome it. But the men that went up with him said, we be not able to go up against the people; for they are stronger than we. And they brought up an evil report of the land which they had searched unto the children of Israel, saying, The land, through which we have gone to search it, is a land that eateth up the inhabitants thereof; and all the people that we saw in it are men of a great stature. And there we saw the giants, the sons of Anak, which come of the giants: and we were in our own sight as grasshoppers, and so we were in their sight. (Numbers 13:25–33).

God gave them a promise, but they allowed what they saw to determine if they can possess what God already told them was theirs. They allowed the giants to limit God's power and ability to carry out His will and plan.

"Now unto him that is able to do exceeding abundantly above all that we ask or think, according to the power that worketh in us" (Ephesians 3:20).

God is able and willing to do more than we ask or think further more we can't think or speak higher enough to challenge what God can do. All what God wants and desires from us is to believe Him, trust Him, and watch Him perform His Word.

"But Jesus beheld them, and said unto them, with men this is impossible; but with God all things are possible" (Matthew 19:26).

"Behold, I am the Lord, the God of all flesh: is there anything too hard for me?" (Jeremiah 32:27)

These are promises from God that we can expect these things in our lives if we believe it.

"Jesus said unto him, if thou canst believe, all things are possible to him that believeth" (Mark 9:23).

If you see all things are possible to whom? To whom that believeth. When you are faced with a limit that I guarantee you this world has set, someone you know has set, or a family member has set when you are removing limitations, you are going against the grain. It's important for you to know when you go against the grain, that alone will cause opposition, criticism, and persecution, but you have to have a made-up mind. Despite all that might be said or done against you, you have to refuse to live the average life when God has made many more promises available to you.

> And it came to pass on a certain day, as he was teaching, that there were Pharisees and doctors of the law sitting by, which were come out of every town of Galilee, and Judaea, and Jerusalem: and the power of the Lord was present to heal them. And, behold, men brought in a bed a man, which was taken with palsy: and they sought means to bring him in, and to lay him before him. And when they could not find by what way they might bring him in because of the multitude, they went upon the housetop, and let him down through the tiling with his couch into the midst before Jesus. And when he saw their faith, he said unto him, Man, thy sins are forgiven thee. (Luke 5:17–20)

Those men were determined to get their friend in there with Jesus, and because they had determination, that determined attitude caused them to move past the limits where others couldn't get in. A no-limit attitude will always cause the wisdom of God to show you another way.

Your only limitation is your imagination. That's why association is critical and vital to your future because it's not necessarily the people that make your future. It's the mindset and the limitation in their thinking that you subject yourself to, to cause that same reality to be in your life.

There is a saying that I learned years ago that says if you can't conceive it, you can't receive it. In other words, if you can't get a mental image of it and see yourself achieving or obtaining it, you will never be able to have it in your hands.

This breakthrough-thinking book is for those who are just tired of going through the same routines in life, in church, on the job, in the marriage, and in every area of life. Because the truth is, life was designed to dictate your life. When you became a born-again child of God, life no longer has the right to dictate what you can or cannot do. That was the greatest problem, the Pharisees, Sadducees, and all the religious people had with Jesus. Jesus did not let them confine Him to their rule, why? Because He knew who He was, and He knew what power He had available to Him. He also understood it was them that was limited and hindered but not Him. It's so important that you know who you are not in a prideful way, but in the way of humility that you don't have to do what everyone else does because you understand that "greater is He that is in me than he that is in the world."

Your victory always starts on the inside before it manifests on the outside. But it is all about what information you are feeding yourself with. Are you feeding yourself with victorious speech, reading, or thinking that you will never accomplished anything, having a positive mentality, or are you feeding yourself with how hard things are, saying that no one in your family has ever accomplished their dreams, or you don't have enough education for that position, the list can go on and on, a limited mindset. And so many people accept what's been said versus having a determined attitude that you are not going to let anything stop or hinder you from fulfilling your calling, the dream you have in your heart and the desire that burns within you. No limits, no boundaries, not only can I see increase all around me, but I decree (speak) increase all around me I decree increase in every area of my life and more is being attracted to me everyday. Environments can set limits, by what you are continually looking at and talking about and by other people low expectations by listening to them; and making you think, "What's the use?" To breakthrough in your thinking, you will have to surround yourself with people with a desire to learn. People understand that the outcome of their lives will not come out the sky; it's going to come about by what you put in it. Stick with the process in spite of what you don't see even if its not happening quick enough.

# CHAPTER 7

# The Power and Purpose of Understanding

In this chapter I'm going to share with you a very vital and critical key to breakthrough thinking. This is something that is overlooked and not much attention has been paid to it. To the people that have understanding are the people you often find doing and accomplishing things that a lot of other people will not give thought to. For example, what makes a good pilot? He understands all that's involved in effectively flying an airplane from the laws of gravity, to the laws of lift, and to reading the compasses, and the interesting thing about it all is that he can't go by sight because when he is ten thousand feet in the air, what is he going to look at, to tell what's around him, especially when going through the clouds. So the pilot has to depend on his level of understanding and his knowledge of what he has been taught. I want to impart that statement of what he has been taught because there is no understanding if you have not been taught. According to what you have been taught is the understanding you will have, good or bad and positive or negative. I have discovered this being a Pastor and coming into contact with so many people from different backgrounds, different environments, and different ways to living life altogether. It took me years to finally realize it's not so much of troubled people. It's their thinking, and the understand-

PASTOR ANTHONY J. STEPHENSON

ing they have about certain things to cause them to act and react to certain things.

Until you change a person thinking, they can't have a changed life. That's why I came to a place even with the church that I Pastor, not to go about it the traditional way of doing things, no offense or anything concerning how others may do, this is because this is what God showed me and instructed me to do. It is to work on their minds while He works on their hearts, Because people can have hard hearts and until they get a certain understanding, their heart will remain hard

"Therefore my people are gone into captivity, because they have no knowledge: and their honorable men are famished, and their multitude dried up with thirst" (Isaiah 5:13).

"My people are destroyed for lack of knowledge: because thou hast rejected knowledge, I will also reject thee, that thou shalt be no priest to me: seeing thou hast forgotten the law of thy God, I will also forget thy children" (Hosea 4:6).

God said that his people are destroyed, cut off from the promises of God because they lacked knowledge, and some have rejected knowledge. This is a very interesting statement made by God, the creator of heaven and earth. First, he said, "My people are destroyed because they lacked knowledge."

"Talk no more so exceeding proudly; let not arrogance come out of your mouth: for the Lord is a God of knowledge, and by him actions are weighed" (1 Samuel 2:3).

It is God's will for you to know so you won't be destroyed. Second, he said some have rejected knowledge. "Poverty and shame shall be to him that refuseth instruction: but he that regardeth reproof shall be honoured" (Proverbs 13:18).

So there again, consequences come from refusing instruction (knowledge and understanding). Understanding can come down to life-or-death situation, so this is not some subject that must be taken lightly and treated as if it's no big deal.

"Get wisdom, get understanding: forget it not; neither decline from the words of my mouth. Forsake her not, and she shall preserve thee: love her, and she shall keep thee. Wisdom is the principal thing;

38

therefore get wisdom: and with all thy getting get understanding. Exalt her, and she shall promote thee: she shall bring thee to honour, when thou dost embrace her" (Proverbs 4:5–8).

"A wise man will hear, and will increase learning; and a man of understanding shall attain unto wise counsels" (Proverbs 1:5)

"And of the children of Issachar, which were men that had understanding of the times, to know what Israel ought to do; the heads of them were two hundred; and all their brethren were at their commandment" (1 Chronicles 12:32).

It has never been God's will for you not to know what to do. That's why the Bible was written; he gave us the Holy Spirit as our helper, and the five-fold ministry, the apostles, prophets, evangelists, pastors, and teachers. So we will not be ignorant of Satan's devices. Why? So whenever you come up against a challenge or the trials of life knocks at your door, you will know what to do. Most mental battles and illness comes from a person constantly thinking about the problem and never getting a solution, so it causes them to turn to whatever that will alter those thoughts for a while until it wears off; and the process starts all over again.

> Turn, O backsliding children, saith the Lord; for I am married unto you: and I will take you one of a city, and two of a family, and I will bring you to Zion: And I will give you pastors according to mine heart, which shall feed you with knowledge and understanding. And it shall come to pass, when ye be multiplied and increased in the land, in those days, saith the Lord, they shall say no more, The ark of the covenant of the Lord: neither shall it come to mind: neither shall they remember it; neither shall they visit it; neither shall that be done any more. (Jeremiah 3:14–16)

Notice the first thing God told them what He was going to do, bring them to Zion (the church). Then He said He would give them pastors according to His heart that will feed them with knowledge and understanding. This is the order of God. Now we also know and are aware that every pastor is not from God, just like you have in other occupations where they are not all on the straight and narrow. But when you know you have a pastor that has the heart of God, his main objective is to teach you about Jesus, the kingdom, and how to walk and live in the love of God.

"Trust in the Lord with all thine heart; and lean not unto thine own understanding" (Proverbs 3:5). To lean on and rely on your own understanding will and can cause you much trouble and harm.

"There is a way which seemeth right unto a man, but the end thereof are the ways of death" (Proverbs 14:12).

And that's what happens when you lean to your own understanding; it seems right because you are looking at it through the mindset that has been developed in you instead of the Wisdom of God.

And to you as a human being, your way has been taught to be the best way regardless, and that's why you hear people say, "That's the way I have always been, and I'm not changing it for you." A mindset that refuses to change is a life that cannot or will not experience change.

> My son, if thou wilt receive my words, and hide my commandments with thee; So that thou incline thine ear unto wisdom, and apply thine heart to understanding; Yea, if thou criest after knowledge, and liftest up thy voice for understanding; If thou seekest her as silver, and searchest for her as for hid treasures; Then shalt thou understand the fear of the Lord, and find the knowledge of God. For the Lord giveth wisdom: out of his mouth cometh knowledge and understanding. (Proverbs 2:1–6)

This is why Satan tries to keep understanding away from you because the more you understand, the greater impact you will make in life and the greater that God will get the glory out of your life.

> That people may know skillful and godly wisdom and instruction, discern and comprehend the words of understanding and insight, Receive instruction in wise dealing and the discipline of wise thoughtfulness, righteousness, justice, and integrity, That prudence may be given to the simple, and knowledge, discretion, and discernment to the youth– The wise also will hear and increase in learning, and the person of understanding will acquire skill and attain to sound counsel [so that he may be able to steer his course rightly]– [Proverbs. 9:9]. (Proverbs 1:2–5 AMP)

The person of understanding will acquire or become skilled at what they do and will have sound, strong, and solid wisdom that they may be able to steer the course of their life rightly. In other words, make good decisions and wise choices.

"Consider what I say; and the Lord give thee understanding in all things" (2 Timothy 2:7). As you can see, the Lord wants us to have understanding in all things. But as understanding will come, the more you are able to be taught, and the more you go after wisdom, knowledge, and understanding through learning from others, reading meditation, praying, and making the life you desire and God's way a priority, which Jesus called the greatest need.

"He that hath knowledge spareth his words: and a man of understanding is of an excellent spirit. Even a fool, when he holdeth his peace, is counted wise: and he that shutteth his lips is esteemed a man of understanding" (Proverbs 17:27–28).

"He that getteth wisdom loveth his own soul: he that keepeth understanding shall find good" (Proverbs 19:8).

"Counsel in the heart of man is like deep water; but a man of understanding will draw it out" (Proverbs 20:5).

> And when he was gone forth into the way, there came one running, and kneeled to him, and asked him, Good Master, what shall I do that

I may inherit eternal life? And Jesus said unto him, Why callest thou me good? There is none good but one, that is, God. Thou knowest the commandments, Do not commit adultery, Do not kill, Do not steal, Do not bear false witness, Defraud not, Honour thy father and mother. And he answered and said unto him, Master, all these have I observed from my youth. Then Jesus beholding him loved him, and said unto him, One thing thou lackest: go thy way, sell whatsoever thou hast, and give to the poor, and thou shalt have treasure in heaven: and come, take up the cross, and follow me. And he was sad at that saying, and went away grieved: for he had great possessions. (Mark 10:17–22)

A lack of understanding will cause you not to trust God because when you lack understanding of the covenant of God, and how God has bound himself obligated himself to His Word. He will move heaven and earth to bring one Word to pass. When He asks you for something, it's something greater that comes in return. But if you don't know Him or His commitment to His Word, whatever He ask you to do, it will be hard for you to do it, or you won't do it because you can't see the benefit on your part behind it.

"The heart of him that hath understanding seeketh knowledge: but the mouth of fools feedeth on foolishness" (Proverbs 15:14).

This is the difference maker right here. The heart and mind of Him that has understanding seeks knowledge, always looking for ways to make their life better through knowledge and understanding, but some conversations of people feeds on foolishness; That's all they talk about, think about, but don't surround themselves with anything that benefits them mentally. And this is for all types of people on every level of life.

That's why I have a great, deep desire to help and develop the inner image of a person who feels less than or that person that was made to feel like they won't accomplish anything or that young woman who may have made a mistake and never was forgiven. Or that person is someone who went to school but couldn't learn as fast as the other kids and made them feel as if they wasn't smart enough and would never be able to do anything worthwhile.

I have written this book to bring hope, encouragement, strength, wisdom, understanding, enlightenment, and different views to all types of people in life. Make today the first day you will walk in the wisdom of God, the knowledge of Him, and the understanding in every area of your life every day.

# CHAPTER 8

# The Power of Confessions

With this chapter, I want to really bring to you the greatest assets to any change, any breakthrough or deliverance. It is called the power of positive confession.

Several years ago there were a powerful book out called the *Power of Positive Thinking* by Dr. Norman Vincent Peale, and he dealt with the importance of not allowing negative thinking to be in your mind because it is eventually going to be in your life.

When we were taught morals and values, and all born into this natural world, we are taught how to feel, and how to express ourselves. Be honest with yourself. In other words, sometimes we let our emotions rule us. That's mostly the problem in the body of Christ; there is hardly any death to self. If anything, it promotes feelings and emotions over the Word of God, not realizing with your mouth you can change anything, any feeling, and any emotion because if salvation came by confession with your mouth and believing in heart, you shall be saved. If those two components have enough power in itself to give you a new nature altogether and change your eternal destination, it can definitely change anything in this natural world. Even God had a plan for Joshua. There was a part Joshua had to play to be fulfilled and carry out that plan. In other words, work with God. "This book of the law shall not depart out of thy mouth; but thou shalt meditate therein day and night, that thou mayest observe to do according to all that is written therein: for then thou shalt make thy way prosperous, and then thou shalt have good success" (Joshua 1:8).

The power of meditation is a powerful thing, and the interesting part of it all, we have all been taught meditation but from the negative side called worry. What do you do when you are worried about something? Your mind is constantly working. You have visions of things taken away from you, and there is no peace of mind. Now meditation on the positive is the exact same thing, but you put your mind on the promises of God and start seeing yourself with that promise no matter how it looks or feels on the outside, you know it's yours. That house is yours, that peace is yours, whatever you are believing God for it is yours. Even for your children salvation and that they are protected and covered under the blood of Jesus. No weapon formed against you shall prosper.

"Blessed is the man that walketh not in the counsel of the ungodly, nor standeth in the way of sinners, nor sitteth in the seat of the scornful. But his delight is in the law of the Lord; and in his law doth he meditate day and night. And he shall be like a tree planted by the rivers of water, that bringeth forth his fruit in his season; his leaf also shall not wither; and whatsoever he doeth shall prosper" (Psalms 1:1–3).

The power of association has more to do with your daily conversation than you realize because you will conform to the environment you continually surround yourself around. It's a universal law that means it goes for everyone in any area of life. So when you are looking for a break-through in your thinking, consider what you are around and who you are around it will make all the difference in the world.

The very first thing I need to know is "For I am not ashamed of the gospel of Christ: for it is the power of God unto salvation to everyone that believeth; to the Jew first, and also to the Greek" (Romans 1:16).

The gospel, the Word of God is the power of God. We must say this over and over again until we really get this in our heart.

The second thing we need to know and understand is "Heaven and earth shall pass away, but my words shall not pass away" (Matthew 24:35).

"So shall my word be that goeth forth out of my mouth: it shall not return unto me void, but it shall accomplish that which I please, and it shall prosper in the thing whereto I sent it" (Isaiah 55:11).

God makes a promise that heaven and earth shall pass away but not His Word, and then He goes on to say that any Word that comes out of His mouth, that Word will not return back to Him in void, in vain, or be unproductive. So far as you can see, the Word of God is the power of God. Everything that we see will pass away except for the Word of God.

Third thing we need to know is "Bless the Lord, ye his angels, that excel in strength, that do his commandments, hearkening unto the voice of his word" (Psalms 103:20).

All of the angelic being has been assigned to hearken, get to attention, and ready to move at the voice of His Word. Now what makes that so awesome and powerful are all the angelic being can't move and go to work unless voice is put to the Word of God. So it's not enough to say how powerful the preaching or teachings is until voice is put to it.

"The centurion answered and said, Lord, I am not worthy that thou shouldest come under my roof: but speak the word only, and my servant shall be healed. For I am a man under authority, having soldiers under me: and I say to this man, Go, and he goeth; and to another, Come, and he cometh; and to my servant, Do this, and he doeth it" (Matthew 8:8–9)

Because this man knows how authority works, he knew Jesus's words are as powerful as His presence. And that's the place the body of Christ will have to get to and know His Word is just as powerful today than it was two thousand years ago. His Word is still healing the sick, opening the blind eyes, and setting the captives free.

It is the will of God that you be free in every area of your life, spirit, soul, body, and mind and in your finances, emotions, and every area.

"Beloved, I wish above all things that thou mayest prosper and be in health, even as thy soul prospereth" (3 John 1:2). But daily confession of the word is a necessity not an option if you want a breakthrough in your life.

Go to the Word and find scriptures that pertain to whatever areas you're standing in agreement with. Stay with it no matter how tough it may seem, and no matter how long it seems you have been waiting, always remember you've got a promise from God, not a man.

"God is not a man, that he should lie; neither the son of man, that he should repent: hath he said, and shall he not do it? Or hath he spoken, and shall he not make it good?" (Numbers 23:19).

Also, God is ready and alert, watching His Word and waiting for someone to put it in their mouth and release it in faith.

"Then said the Lord to me, you have seen well, for I am alert and active, watching over my word to perform it" (Jeremiah 1:12 AMP).

"This book of the law shall not depart out of thy mouth; but thou shalt meditate therein day and night, that thou mayest observe to do according to all that is written therein: for then thou shalt make thy way prosperous, and then thou shalt have good success" (Joshua 1:8).

What you give your mind and your attention to is what will manifest in your life.

Here are some examples to get you started on the road to success.

# CHAPTER 9

# Daily Confessions

I set the course of my life today with my words:

> I declare today that I will not be defeated, discouraged, depressed or disappointed today.
>
> I am the head, I have insight, I have wisdom, I have ideas, and I have authority.
>
> I exercise my authority today with my words and I decree a thing and it is so.
>
> Greater is He that is in me than he that is in the world (1 John 4:4) . . . the same Spirit that raised Jesus from the dead, lives in me . . . (Romans 8:11)
>
> As I speak words today, they come to pass (Job 22:28); they go before me, they bring the things to pass that I desire; and they stop all attacks, assaults, oppression, and fear from coming to my life.
>
> God is on my side today and, therefore, I cannot be defeated.
>
> His favor surrounds me today as a shield. (Psalms 5:12) I expect favor today from heaven and from the earth.

Jesus had favor with God and man (Luke 2:52), and as He is so am I on this earth (1 John 4:17) Therefore, I have favor today with God and man.

I expect and receive favor in my home, favor on my job, favor in my business, favor in my ministry, favor with my finances, and favor in every deal I am involved in.

I have the wisdom of God today. I will think the right thoughts, say the right words and make the right decisions in every situation I face today.

My mouth speaks wisdom and my heart is filled with understanding. (Psalm 49:3)

I ask for, and receive, an abundant supply of wisdom and understanding today from God (James 1:5)…wisdom from above, wisdom that is pure, peaceable, gentle, unwavering, willing to yield, without hypocrisy. (James 3:17)

Wisdom and understanding are better than silver and gold and nothing I desire can compare with them; therefore, I make it my ambition and desire to have understanding and wisdom; therefore I know I will have all of the other desires of my heart. (Proverbs 8:10-11)

My words go before me in securing my divine health and healing…

I will not be sick today; I will not be sad today; I will not be broke today; I will not be confused today.

I have health today; I have joy today; I have all the money I need in the name of Jesus.

The Lord orders my steps… (Psalm 37:23)

I have a covenant with God and by the blood of Jesus I release my divine protection and divine provision.

My angels are carrying out the Word of God on my behalf.

I receive supernatural strength and encouragement from God and my angels. Angels carry out the Word of God and angels are carrying out every word that I speak that line up with the Word of God, even now as I speak. (Psalm 103:20)

I expect to have divine appointments today, to run into the right people, and to be delivered from the wrong people.

Any adversity, attack, accidents and tragedies that were headed my way are diverted right now in Jesus' name.

I speak to the raging waters in my life: Peace, be still.

I say to my emotions, peace, be still.

I say to my mind, peace, be still.

I say to my body, peace, be still.

I say to my home, peace, be still.

I say to my family, peace, be still.

Now I speak to: every mountain of fear, every mountain of discouragement, every mountain of stress, every mountain of depression, every mountain of lack and insufficiency.

And I say, "Be removed and cast into the sea in Jesus' name!" (Mark 11:23) I expect the best day of my life spiritually, emotionally, relationally and financially today in Jesus' name! (Quoted by Gregory Dickow)

# CHAPTER 10

# The Purpose and Power of the Local Church

This is one of the most misunderstood and deceptive topics that Satan has brought to the children of God. Without a true real biblical answer, this is part of your Christian walk which is in my consideration the most important thing you must be part of after receiving Jesus as Lord of your life.

After you receive Jesus as Lord of your life, a whole new life begins, but this life that you are now beginning to live is a whole new way of living that you will have to be taught how to live it. It's totally different from the system of this world. In the past here, few years there, they have been a great falling away of the local church, which is one of the traps Satan uses.

Hosea 4:1; 6, Isaiah 5:13, both of these came as a result of lack of knowledge and no knowledge, so what you know is critical to how you will live.

> Turn, O backsliding children, saith the Lord; for I am married unto you: and I will take you one of a city, and two of a family, and I will bring you to Zion: And I will give you pastors according to mine heart, which shall feed you with knowledge and understanding. And it shall come to

pass, when ye be multiplied and increased in the land, in those days, saith the Lord, they shall say no more, The ark of the covenant of the Lord: neither shall it come to mind: neither shall they remember it; neither shall they visit it; neither shall that be done any more. (Jeremiah 3:14–16)

You know this must be a serious thing for God to make it a priority, (*see* Acts 2:36-47).

The first church of the New Testament showed and demonstrated the power and purpose of the local church.

- Purpose is the reason for which something is done or created or for which something exists as one's intention or objective.
- Value is the regard that something is held to deserved; the importance, worth, or usefulness of something.
- What you don't value, you won't see the purpose of it, and when you don't see the purpose of it, you won't see the need of it. (It will not be important to you).
- Once this is defined, concerning the purpose and the value of ministry and your local church, you are now held responsible for the growth and increase of it.

God's way is perfect and you will never go wrong going the way he tells you to do it (*see* Psalm 18:30).

This is something that you must be aware of and don't allow it to cause you not to fully obey God by a tradition that you hold on to verses, letting God direct you (*see* Matthew 15:1–6).

Jesus commissioned the disciples to go and make disciples train, equip, and teach others what He taught them (*see* Matthew 28:16–20 AMP

- After receiving salvation (placing Jesus into your Heart), now you have to be taught how to live this Christian life.

- The church is a place where believers come together to come into a greater knowledge and understanding of their covenant and how to live in that covenant in the earth.

My people are in bondage because they have no knowledge (*see* Isaiah 5:13).

My people, God's people, He said are destroyed because they lacked knowledge, but then there are some who reject knowledge, and that refusal of learning he said will cause you not to be a priest to Him (represent) Him (see Hosea 4:6).

God is interested in you, knowing what to do. God is a God of knowledge (*see* 1 Samuel 2:3).

"I will instruct thee and teach thee in the way you should go; I will guide you with my eye" (Psalms 32:8).

And such as do wickedly against the covenant shall he corrupt or deceive, but the people that do know their God shall be strong and do great exploits (great things) (*see* Daniel 11:32).

God has a plan for you that will lead you to the life he ordained for you to live (*see* Jeremiah 29:11 AMP).

Surely the Lord God won't do anything until He reveals it to his servants the prophets (*see* Amos 3:7).

You have three profound ways how God speak to His people:

1. The written Word
2. The rhema (revealed word—Revelation), what you hear within
3) Through spiritual authority (the authority God put in place), pastor, etc.

The purpose of the five-fold ministry and the understanding is that they are gifts from God through Jesus to the body of Christ (*see* Ephesians 4:7–14).

God said He would give you a pastor according to His heart, which shall feed you with knowledge and understanding (*see* Jeremiah 3:14–16).

Your spiritual maturity determines how much of the inheritance you will receive (*see* Galatians 4:1–2).

You determine how fast you grow and develop in your walk of faith.

There can't be any change in any person's life until there is a change in your thinking. And that's why church is so vital and there has been so many attacks on churches, making people believe and think that the church is not needed to have a change in your life, or you don't need a pastor. The big question is why did God put those things in place if He had no need for them? That's been Satan's way of disconnecting people from the body so they can't grow and be all God has intended for them to be.

When you are talking about breakthrough thinking, it's going to take someone who has been where you have never been to take you where you desire to go. Exposure to new things is probably one of the best thing that can happen because your mind and your thinking can be trapped in a box. A box that only you have heard or seen, and those things are the right things even though they can be wrong altogether but because that's all you know, and all that you experience is new, it may or may not be acceptable. It's all about how you think or how you were taught to think.

The church was designed and instituted not so much as it is been used for today. The church is used for so many other things today more than its intended purpose. The church was a place used to gather the saints together to preach the Word to them, heal them, to feed them, and lead them to Jesus. The reason they feed them because there were times they were there all day long, not like the two-hour service today to be convenient to the people. The apostle Paul one time preached all night (*see* Acts 20:7–10). There was no time limit on the Word of God. They were just excited to hear and see what the power of God was doing. Also a very important key is you have control over the atmosphere or environment that is there. A lot of pressure has been and continue to get put on the pastor, praise team, and choir when in reality, if you don't come with no expectations, It does not matter how anointed the pastor is and how awesome the music ministry is. If you don't release your faith and have an expectation, you will leave the same way you came. That's part of the new thinking process that must take place as a believer in Christianity. I will instruct you and teach you the way you should go; and I will guide you with my eye. Psalms 32:8 NKJV

# CHAPTER 11

# Your Future Is in Your Mouth, Partnering with God

In this last chapter of breakthrough thinking, this should sum up all what you have already read. By now, I trust and believe God that you are already seeing the necessity on why renewal of the mind is so important. Jesus said something in Matthew 25:6, "And honour not his father or his mother, he shall be free. Thus have ye made the commandment of God of none effect by your tradition."

Tradition is not the name and the activities of a church, but tradition is a ritual, something that was put together and made it a law. Another definition of tradition is rules handed down from generation to generation without any written instruction. In other words it didn't come from God. So whatever hasn't come from the lips and mouth of God, He is not obligated to perform.

"Then said the Lord to me, you have seen well, for I am alert and active, watching over my word to perform it" (Jeremiah 1:12 AMP)

God watches over His Word to perform it. Now in this disposition, Jesus is our apostle and high priest who watch over our words to bring our words to pass. It's a win-win situation. But religion and tradition will rob you of the abundant life that has already been prepared for us.

It is a wonderful life as a child of God once you get the correct knowledge of His Word and of how to live in this covenant life. But that's what all the mental and physical battles has been over, in and out of our lives, so you can't learn what you need to learn. Change your association because Satan knows you can't go any higher than your surroundings (see Jeremiah 29:11; Proverbs 31:25–31AMP).

A partner is a person who shares or is associated with another in some action or endeavor; a sharer; an associate; a player on the same team.(dictionary.com)

Since we belong to God, He has already promised us concerning our future (see Isaiah 43:1–6, 25–26).

That is God speaking to us too. Our future is bright. God is going before us and making some things right that we may have messed up along the way (see Isaiah 45:1–3, 11–13).

"And the Lord said unto Moses, Depart, and go up hence, thou and the people which thou hast brought up out of the land of Egypt, unto the land which I swore unto Abraham, to Isaac, and to Jacob, saying, Unto thy seed will I give it: And I will send an angel before thee; and I will drive out the Canaanite, the Amorite, and the Hittite, and the Perizzite, the Hivite, and the Jebusite" (Exodus 33:1–2).

> Behold, I send an Angel before thee, to keep thee in the way, and to bring thee into the place which I have prepared. Beware of him, and obey his voice, provoke him not; for he will not pardon your transgressions: for my name is in him. But if thou shalt indeed obey his voice, and do all that I speak; then I will be an enemy unto thine enemies, and an adversary unto thine adversaries. For mine Angel shall go before thee, and bring thee in unto the Amorites, and the Hittites, and the Perizzites, and the Canaanites, the Hivites, and the Jebusites: and I will cut them off. Thou shalt not bow down to their gods, nor serve them, nor do after their works: but thou shalt utterly overthrow them, and quite break down their images. And ye shall serve the Lord your God, and He shall bless thy bread, and thy water;

and I will take sickness away from the midst of thee. There shall nothing cast their young, nor be barren, in thy land: the number of thy days I will fulfill. I will send my fear before thee, and will destroy all the people to whom thou shalt come, and I will make all thine enemies turn their backs unto thee. And I will send hornets before thee, which shall drive out the Hivite, the Canaanite, and the Hittite, from before thee. I will not drive them out from before thee in one year; lest the land become desolate, and the beast of the field multiply against thee. By little and little I will drive them out from before thee, until thou be increased, and inherit the land. And I will set thy bounds from the Red sea even unto the sea of the Philistines, and from the desert unto the river: for I will deliver the inhabitants of the land into your hand; and thou shalt drive them out before thee. Thou shalt make no covenant with them, or with their gods. They shall not dwell in thy land, lest they make thee sin against me: for if thou serve their gods, it will surely be a snare unto thee. (Exodus 23:20–33)

Darkness, void, and emptiness was present but that's not what God wanted, so He changed what He wanted by what He said to it and what He called it (*see* Genesis 1:1–3).

My present and future will be what I call it not what the conditions of the land produce, but what I call it according to the Word of God.

God will not lie, if He said it He will do it; if He spoke it He will make it good. Numbers 23:19

It is impossible for God to lie. He is under obligation to carry out His Word if I believe it and hold him to it (*see* Isaiah 43:25–26; Hebrews 6:18)

His Word will not return to him void, vain, or unproductive (*see* Isaiah 55:11)

With God, nothing is ever impossible and no Word from God shall be without power or impossible of fulfillment (*see* Luke 1:37 AMP).

This centurion understood about authority and how authority works; and that is, a person in authority, whose words are just as powerful as their presence. Jesus's Words were not His, but the Father who sent him (*see* Matthew 8:5–8).

Your mouth will be an instrument, which God will use to bring His will to pass in your life (*see* Isaiah 41:15).

We have been given everything that we need that pertains unto life and godliness (*see* 2 Peter 1:2–4). Verse 4 says we have been given seeds (promises) from God to live by, and those promises will enable us to escape the corruption of this world, giving us as Christians a way out!

The Word is spirit just like God is spirit. God and His Word are one, inseparable (*see* Matthew 4: 4).

When you speak of His word, He is present. Man shall not live by bread alone, physical things by itself; your life is more spiritual than it is physical and that's why the Word of God is a necessity, a must, why? That's how everything came into existence and how it comes into existence is through spirit form (*see* St. John 1:1–3).

1. All things were made, everything is made (good or bad, positive or negative, it was made), and being made (see verse 3(AMP)).
2. Came into existence, or coming into existence past, present, or future.
3. Through Him, by Him or through you by you.

You are the prophet of your own life (*see* 2 Corinthians 6:1). We are responsible for working with God to bring the will of God to pass. God supplies us with His word and power and we supply the faith and the mouth.

How your life will exist and how you spend your days will be based on what's coming out of your mouth. This is so crucial and has been overlooked for generations. God plainly made it known in the very beginning that we have been made in His image and in His likeness. So with that, everything God created and made, he did it with His mouth. All of creation came into existence through his mouth (*see* 1 Peter 3:10; Psalms 34:10–14).

Many people have not made the connection between their life and their words. They were more concerned about eating with unwashed hands but Jesus was trying to get them to understand on what comes out of your mouth; that does more damage than eating with unwashed hands (*see* Matthew 15:10–20).

In Exodus 4:10–15 God promised Moses that He would be with his mouth, and He gave Moses the rod (the Word of God) and that was what he used for the signs and made things happen with.

God confirms His Word with the manifestation of that Word been seen or coming to pass in this physical world (*see* Mark 16:15–20).

"My covenant will I not break, nor alter the thing that is gone out of my lips" (Psalms 89:34). We have a promise from God that God will not break His Word. We can literally base our life on His Word. His Word will never fail.

It's dangerous to speak against the Holy Spirit. Jesus said that would never be forgiven in this world or that to come (*see* Matthew 12:30–32).

Blasphemy is disrespecting the acts and ways of God with words and actions, a negative behavior toward sacred things of God. Your life will come as a result of what you fill your heart up with. The law of overflow is what you constantly fill yourself up with; It will be seen in your individual life or around you (*see* Matthew 12:33–37).

How forcible or powerful are right words, which is the Word of God (*see* Job 6:24–26).

# CHAPTER 12

# The Proverbs of Words and the Power of Them

When you watch what comes out of your mouth, that will save you from a lot of grief (*see* Proverbs 21:23 AMP). So I agree with you right now that the only thing coming out of your mouth is for the good. In your health, finances, promotions, success, wholeness, peace, and salvation for others, there is no lack in your life. There is abundant life and it is so. So rejoice in advance, knowing the perfect will of God has been manifested in your life.

"Again I say unto you, that if two of you shall agree on earth as touching anything that they shall ask, it shall be done for them of my Father which is in heaven. For where two or three are gathered together in my name, there am I in the midst of them" (Matthew 18:19–20).

References: Proverbs 6:2; Proverbs 12:14; Proverbs 13:2–3; Proverbs 16:21–25; Proverbs 18:6–8; Proverbs 20–21.

## ABOUT THE AUTHOR

 Pastor Anthony J. Stephenson is the senior pastor and founder of Life Changing International Church, Incorporated in High Point, North Carolina. He has been serving in ministry for twenty-three years and has been pastoring and teaching and preaching the uncompromised word of God for eighteen years. He teaches the word of God with such simplicity and understanding to better the lives of the people of all ages. It is his desire to see God's word manifested in the lives of the people. He has traveled the world teaching Gods word. He inspires to impact the lives of people through the love of God. His life exemplifies the word he teaches. The spirit of faith and excellence are embedded in the vision God has given him. He has been married for over twenty years to his wife Yolanda who serves along with him in the ministry as well as their three children, one daughter Kanesha, with her husband Tony, and two sons, Anthony Jr., and An'tre. He currently resides in North Carolina.

CPSIA information can be obtained
at www.ICGtesting.com
Printed in the USA
FFOW05n0415031116